sssssssssssShadows in the House

In the quiet suburban neighborhood of Willow Grove, nestled amidst towering trees and manicured lawns, stood the modest yet cozy home of

Marcus, Kate, and Rola. With its welcoming front porch and neatly trimmed hedges, their house exuded an air of warmth and tranquility, a sanctuary from the hustle and bustle of the .outside world

Inside, the atmosphere was one of love and laughter, as Marcus, Kate, and Rola went about their daily routines with a sense of contentment and joy. Marcus, the strong and dependable patriarch of the family, worked tirelessly to provide for his loved ones, while Kate, his devoted wife, tended to the needs of their home with grace and aplomb. And then there was Rola, their bright-eyed and curious daughter, whose infectious laughter filled every corner of their home with happiness.

In these peaceful moments, before the arrival of the zombies, the family's bond was unbreakable, their love for each other a beacon of light in an often-dark world. They shared meals around the kitchen table, went for walks in the nearby park, and spent lazy Sunday afternoons playing games in the backyard.

But beneath the surface of this idyllic existence, there lingered a sense of unease—a feeling that their tranquil life could be shattered at any moment by forces beyond their control. Little did they know that their peaceful existence was about to be violently upended by the arrival of the undead, plunging them into a

nightmare from which there
would be no easy escape.

As the sun set on another ordinary day in Willow Grove, casting long shadows across the peaceful streets, Marcus, Kate, and Rola settled in for the night, unaware of the horrors that awaited them just beyond their doorstep.

The Day Everything **Changed

The morning sun rose lazily over the tranquil

neighborhood of Willow Grove, casting a warm glow over the rows of houses lining the quiet streets. Inside one of these houses, Marcus, Kate, and Rola began their day with the familiar rituals that had come to define their peaceful existence.

The aroma of sizzling bacon and freshly brewed coffee wafted through the air as Marcus, the sturdy patriarch of the family, flipped pancakes on the stove with practiced ease. Kate, his devoted wife, bustled about the kitchen, setting the table with plates and utensils as Rola, their bright-eyed daughter, chattered excitedly about the adventures she .hoped to have that day

As they sat down to breakfast together, the air was filled with laughter and conversation, the simple joys of family life bringing warmth to their hearts. Marcus and Kate shared a knowing glance, their love for each other and their daughter evident in the way they smiled and laughed together, their bond unbreakable even .in the face of adversity

But as the morning wore on, a sense of unease began to settle over the neighborhood, a feeling that something was not quite right. Marcus and Kate exchanged concerned glances as rumors of strange occurrences and unsettling sightings began to spread, whispered conversations echoing through the streets like a dark omen of things to .come

By midday, the whispers had turned to cries of panic as reports of violent attacks and bizarre behavior flooded in from neighboring towns. Marcus and Kate's hearts raced with fear as they realized that whatever was happening was spreading closer and closer to home, threatening to shatter the peace and tranquility they .had come to cherish

As the afternoon sun dipped lower in the sky, casting long shadows across the quiet streets of Willow Grove, the first signs of chaos began to emerge. Screams pierced the air as the dead rose from their graves and the living succumbed to a primal hunger for flesh, their once-familiar faces twisted into grotesque masks of death and decay.

In the blink of an eye, the world as Marcus, Kate, and Rola knew it was gone, replaced by a nightmare of unimaginable horror. With every passing moment, the undead hordes grew larger and more relentless, their bloodcurdling moans echoing through the streets like a chilling symphony of death.

And as darkness descended over Willow Grove, Marcus, Kate, and Rola found themselves standing on the precipice of an abyss, their peaceful existence shattered by the arrival of the undead and their once-tranquil neighborhood transformed into a battleground for survival.

*Survival Instincts

As chaos descended upon Willow Grove like a shroud of darkness, Marcus, Kate, and Rola found themselves thrust into a terrifying new reality. With the undead horde closing in on their home, they were forced to rely on their wits and instincts to .survive

Marcus, drawing on his years of practical experience, took charge of fortifying their house against the impending threat. He hammered boards over windows, reinforced doors with whatever heavy furniture he could find, and stockpiled supplies in preparation for the siege ahead. Every creak of the floorboards and every distant moan from outside sent a shiver down his spine, but he pushed aside his fear, focusing instead on protecting his family at all .costs

Kate, ever the resourceful one, scoured the house for any tools or weapons they could use to defend themselves. She found an old baseball bat in the garage and a set of kitchen knives in the drawer, arming herself with whatever makeshift weapons she could find. With determination etched into her features, she stood ready to fight alongside Marcus, her love for him and Rola giving her the strength to face whatever horrors awaited them outside.

Rola, too young to fully grasp the gravity of the situation, clung to her parents with wide-eyed innocence, her small hands clutching at their clothes as if seeking reassurance. Marcus and Kate did their best to shield her from the grim reality unfolding outside, but they knew that they could not protect her forever. They vowed to do whatever it took to keep her safe, to shield her from the horrors of the world for as long as they could.

As night fell and the sounds of the undead grew louder, Marcus, Kate, and Rola huddled together in the dimly lit living room, their hearts pounding in their chests as they waited for the inevitable onslaught. Outside, the streets were eerily silent, save for the occasional shuffle of footsteps and the distant moans of the undead, a stark reminder of the danger that lurked just .beyond their doorstep

In the darkness of their besieged home, the family clung to each other, their bond stronger than ever in the face of adversity. With every passing moment, they

knew that their survival
depended on their unity, their
love for each other a beacon
of hope in a world consumed
.by darkness

And as they braced
themselves for the long night
ahead, Marcus, Kate, and
Rola vowed to fight for their
lives, to defy the odds and
emerge victorious against
the relentless tide of death
that threatened to consume
.them

**The Siege Begins :

As the first light of dawn broke over Willow Grove, Marcus, Kate, and Rola braced themselves for the onslaught they knew was coming. The air was thick with tension as they listened intently for any sign of movement outside, every creak of the floorboards and every rustle of leaves setting .their nerves on edge

Suddenly, a low, guttural moan echoed through the stillness, sending a chill down their spines. The undead horde had arrived, drawn by the scent of the living within the barricaded walls of their home.

With hearts pounding, Marcus and Kate took their positions at the windows, ready to defend their home against the approaching threat. Kate gripped the baseball bat tightly in her hands, her knuckles turning white with tension, while Marcus peered through a crack In the boarded-up window, his eyes scanning the horizon for any sign of movement.

Outside, the zombies shuffled closer, their vacant eyes fixed on the house like predators stalking their prey. Marcus and Kate tensed, their breath caught in their throats as the first of the undead slammed against the barricades, their groans mingling with the sound of .splintering wood

With a roar of defiance, Marcus swung open the window and lunged forward, striking out at the nearest zombie with all his strength.

Kate followed suit, her bat connecting with a sickening thud as she fended off the advancing horde.

Meanwhile, Rola huddled in a corner of the room, her eyes wide with fear as she watched her parents fight off the undead. Though she was terrified, she knew that she had to stay strong for their sake, to be brave in the face of unimaginable danger.

For hours, the siege raged on, the undead relentless in their pursuit of the living.

Marcus and Kate fought with every ounce of strength they possessed, their bodies aching and bruised from the constant onslaught. But still, they refused to give up, their determination to protect their family unwavering in the face .of overwhelming odds

Just when it seemed that all hope was lost, a sudden noise echoed through the house—a roar of engines and the sound of gunfire. Marcus and Kate exchanged bewildered glances, their hearts pounding with a mixture of fear and hope.

And then, like a ray of sunshine breaking through the clouds, a group of survivors burst through the streets, armed to the teeth and ready to lend a hand in the fight against the undead. With renewed vigor, Marcus, Kate, and their newfound allies rallied together, their combined strength turning the tide of battle in their favor.

As the last of the zombies fell, defeated by the combined efforts of the survivors, Marcus, Kate, and Rola breathed a sigh of relief, their bodies weary but their spirits unbroken. Though they knew that the fight was far from over, they took comfort in the knowledge that they were not alone—that together, they could overcome any obstacle that stood in their way.

And so, as the sun set on another day in Willow Grove,

Marcus, Kate, and Rola stood united, their bond stronger than ever in the face of adversity. Though the road ahead would be long and treacherous, they knew that as long as they had each other, they could face whatever challenges the future held with courage and determination.

: The Siege Begins**

As the first light of dawn broke over Willow Grove, Marcus, Kate, and Rola braced themselves for the onslaught they knew was coming. The air was thick with tension as they listened intently for any sign of movement outside, every creak of the floorboards and every rustle of leaves setting their nerves on edge.

Suddenly, a low, guttural moan echoed through the stillness, sending a chill down their spines. The undead horde had arrived, drawn by the scent of the living within the barricaded walls of their home.

With hearts pounding, Marcus and Kate took their positions at the windows, ready to defend their home against the approaching threat. Kate gripped the baseball bat tightly in her hands, her knuckles turning white with tension, while Marcus peered through a crack in the boarded-up window, his eyes scanning the horizon for any sign of movement.

Outside, the zombies shuffled closer, their vacant eyes fixed on the house like predators stalking their prey. Marcus and Kate tensed, their breath caught in their throats as the first of the undead slammed against the barricades, their groans mingling with the sound of splintering wood.

With a roar of defiance, Marcus swung open the window and lunged forward, striking out at the nearest zombie with all his strength. Kate followed suit, her bat connecting with a sickening thud as she fended off the advancing horde.

Meanwhile, Rola huddled in a corner of the room, her eyes wide with fear as she watched her parents fight off the undead. Though she was terrified, she knew that she had to stay strong for their sake, to be brave in the face of unimaginable danger.

For hours, the siege raged on, the undead relentless in their pursuit of the living. Marcus and Kate fought with every ounce of strength they possessed, their bodies aching and bruised from the constant onslaught. But still, they refused to give up, their determination to protect their family unwavering in the face of overwhelming odds.

Just when it seemed that all hope was lost, a sudden noise echoed through the house—a roar of engines and the sound of gunfire. Marcus and Kate exchanged bewildered glances, their hearts pounding with a mixture of fear and hope.

And then, like a ray of sunshine breaking through the clouds, a group of survivors burst through the streets, armed to the teeth and ready to lend a hand in the fight against the undead. With renewed vigor, Marcus, Kate, and their newfound allies rallied together, their combined strength turning the tide of battle in their favor.

As the last of the zombies fell, defeated by the combined efforts of the survivors, Marcus, Kate, and Rola breathed a sigh of relief, their bodies weary but their spirits unbroken. Though they knew that the fight was far from over, they took comfort in the knowledge that they were not alone—that together, they could overcome any obstacle that stood in their way.

And so, as the sun set on another day in Willow Grove, Marcus, Kate, and Rola stood united, their bond stronger than ever in the face of adversity. Though the road ahead would be long and treacherous, they knew that as long as they had each other, they could face whatever challenges the future held with courage and determination.

____

____

: The Search for Safety**

With the immediate threat of the undead horde vanquished, Marcus, Kate, Rola, and their newfound allies set out on a perilous journey in search of safety and sanctuary. Every step they took was fraught with danger, every shadow hiding a potential threat, but they pressed on, driven by the hope of finding a place where they could rebuild their lives free from fear and uncertainty.

Their path led them through the desolate streets of Willow Grove, where the remnants of civilization lay in ruins. Buildings smoldered and streets were littered with debris, a grim reminder of the devastation wrought by the zombie apocalypse. The once-thriving neighborhood now lay silent and empty, haunted by the echoes of the past.

As they ventured further from home, the group encountered other survivors, each with their own stories of loss and survival. Some welcomed them with open arms, offering food and shelter in exchange for their help in fortifying their defenses against the undead. Others viewed them with suspicion, their trust hard-earned and easily lost in a world where betrayal lurked around every corner.

Despite the dangers that surrounded them, Marcus, Kate, and Rola found strength in their bond as a family, drawing courage from each other as they navigated the treacherous terrain of the zombie-infested world. They clung to hope like a lifeline, refusing to give in to despair even in the face of overwhelming odds.

Along the way, they encountered both friend and foe, their journey marked by moments of triumph and tragedy. They fought off hordes of zombies, braved treacherous landscapes, and forged alliances with other survivors, all in the name of finding a place where they

could finally lay down their
weapons and call home.

But as they ventured deeper into the unknown, they soon realized that the road ahead would be far more perilous than they had ever imagined. With each passing mile, they came face to face with the harsh realities of life in a world overrun by the undead—a world where danger lurked around every corner and death could strike at any moment.

Yet still, they pressed on, fueled by the hope of finding a place where they could finally find peace and safety. For Marcus, Kate, and Rola, the journey was far from over, but they knew that as long as they had each other, they could face whatever challenges the future held with courage and determination.

And so, as they ventured into the unknown, Marcus, Kate, and Rola held tight to each other, their hearts filled with hope and their spirits unbroken in the face of adversity. For in a world consumed by darkness, their love for each other was the light that guided them through the darkest of times.

**A Glint of Hope :

As the weary travelers pressed on through the desolate landscape, their spirits weighed heavy with the burdens of their journey, a glimmer of hope appeared on the horizon. In the distance, rising like a beacon of light in the darkness, stood the silhouette of a fortified settlement—a sanctuary amidst the chaos .of the zombie-infested world

With renewed determination, Marcus, Kate, Rola, and their companions quickened their pace, their hearts pounding with anticipation as they drew closer to their destination. Every step brought them closer to safety, every breath filled with the promise of a new .beginning

As they neared the settlement, they were met by

a group of guards, armed and vigilant in their defense of the enclave. Marcus stepped forward, his hands raised in a gesture of peace, as he explained their plight and begged for sanctuary within the walls of the .settlement

The guards eyed them warily, their expressions guarded as they assessed the newcomers before them. But as Marcus spoke of their journey and the trials they had endured, a spark of compassion flickered in their

eyes, and they nodded in
.understanding

With a sense of relief washing over them, Marcus, Kate, Rola, and their companions were welcomed into the safety of the settlement, their weary bodies finding respite within its sturdy walls. Here, amidst the hustle and bustle of daily life, they found a sense of community and belonging .they had thought long lost

But even as they settled into their new home, the specter

of danger loomed large on the horizon. For outside the safety of the settlement walls, the undead still roamed, a constant reminder of the fragile peace they had found within.

Yet despite the ever-present threat of danger, Marcus, Kate, and Rola felt a glimmer of hope stirring within their hearts. For In this fortified enclave, surrounded by allies and friends, they knew that they had finally found a place where they could begin to rebuild their lives and reclaim

their humanity in a world
consumed by darkness.

And as they looked to the future with newfound optimism, Marcus, Kate, Rola, and their companions vowed to stand together, united in their determination to forge a brighter tomorrow amidst the shadows of the apocalypse.

Battleground of the Undead

Within the safety of the settlement walls, Marcus,

Kate, Rola, and their companions found themselves faced with a new set of challenges. While the enclave offered sanctuary from the dangers of the outside world, it was not without its own perils, chief among them the constant threat of undead attacks.

As night fell over the settlement, the air grew thick with tension as the sound of moaning filled the air—the telltale sign of an approaching horde of zombies. Marcus, Kate, and

Rola joined their fellow survivors on the front lines, their weapons at the ready as they prepared to defend their home against the relentless onslaught.

With a roar of defiance, the undead horde descended upon the settlement, their numbers overwhelming as they crashed against the fortified walls like a tidal wave of death. Marcus and Kate fought side by side, their movements fluid and precise as they struck down zombie after zombie, their hearts pounding with adrenaline as they battled to protect their family and friends.

Rola, though young, proved herself a formidable fighter, her small frame darting through the chaos as she delivered swift blows to the undead with surprising skill and agility. With every swing of her weapon, she fought with a ferocity born of desperation, her determination unwavering in the face of overwhelming odds.

As the battle raged on, the settlement's defenders fought with a unity born of necessity, their movements coordinated and precise as they held the line against the relentless tide of death. Yet for every zombie they struck down, it seemed two more took its place, their numbers seemingly endless in their quest to overwhelm the living.

But just when It seemed that all hope was lost, a deafening roar echoed through the night—a sound that struck fear into the hearts of the undead and brought renewed hope to the defenders of the settlement. For on the horizon, a group of reinforcements appeared, armed to the teeth and ready to lend their aid in the fight against the undead.

With fresh resolve, Marcus, Kate, Rola, and their companions rallied together, their spirits lifted by the arrival of their newfound allies. Together, they fought with a renewed sense of purpose, pushing back against the horde with all their strength and determination.

And as the first light of dawn broke over the horizon, the last of the undead fell, defeated by the combined efforts of the settlement's defenders. With weary but triumphant smiles, Marcus, Kate, Rola, and their companions surveyed the battlefield, their hearts filled with pride and gratitude for each other's bravery and sacrifice.

For in the crucible of combat, they had forged bonds that could never be broken, their unity a testament to the resilience of the human spirit in the face of unimaginable adversity. And as they stood together amidst the ruins of battle, they knew that no matter what trials lay ahead, they would face them with courage and determination, united in their quest for survival and hope for a better tomorrow.

**Shadows of Betrayal :

In the aftermath of the fierce battle against the undead, a tense calm settled over the settlement. The air was heavy with the scent of blood and sweat, the echoes of combat still ringing in the ears of the survivors. But amidst the rubble and wreckage, darker forces began to stir, threatening to unravel the fragile peace that had been so hard-won.

As the settlement's defenders tended to their wounds and mourned their fallen comrades, whispers of discontent began to spread among the survivors. Rumors of betrayal and treachery circulated like wildfire, casting a shadow of suspicion over those who had once fought side by side.

Among the survivors, tensions simmered beneath the surface, fueled by fear and uncertainty. Old rivalries flared anew, and alliances once thought unbreakable began to crumble under the weight of suspicion and mistrust.

But it was not just whispers and rumors that threatened to tear the settlement apart. As the days passed, a series of mysterious incidents began to occur—supplies went missing, weapons disappeared, and guards reported sightings of shadowy figures lurking in the darkness beyond the .settlement walls

At first, these incidents were dismissed as the result of paranoia and exhaustion, the byproduct of living in a world ravaged by death and decay. But as the evidence mounted and tensions reached a boiling point, it became clear that something more sinister .was at play

As night fell over the settlement, Marcus, Kate, Rola, and their companions found themselves drawn into a web of intrigue and deception, their loyalties tested like never before. With danger lurking around every corner, they were forced to confront the harsh reality that not everyone within the settlement could be trusted.

And as the shadows closed in around them, Marcus, Kate, Rola, and their companions realized that if they were to survive in this treacherous new world, they would need to rely on each other more than ever before. For in the face of betrayal and deceit, their bond as a family would be their greatest strength—and their only hope for survival.

Unraveling Secrets:

As tensions simmered within the settlement, Marcus, Kate, Rola, and their companions found themselves thrust into a desperate race against time to uncover the truth behind the mysterious incidents plaguing their newfound home. With suspicion and mistrust tearing at the fabric of their community, they knew that they could trust no one but each other as they delved deeper into the shadows of betrayal.

Their investigation led them down a twisting path of secrets and lies, as they unearthed long-buried truths that threatened to shatter the fragile peace of the settlement. They questioned their fellow survivors, piecing together fragments of information in their quest for answers, but with each revelation came only more questions, and the truth remained elusive.

But as they dug deeper, Marcus, Kate, Rola, and their companions began to uncover a sinister plot that threatened not only their own safety but the very survival of the settlement itself. They discovered that a faction of disgruntled survivors, driven by greed and ambition, had been secretly hoarding supplies and weapons, sowing discord and dissent in their quest for power.

With the fate of the settlement hanging in the balance, Marcus, Kate, Rola, and their companions knew that they could not stand idly by while their home was torn apart from within. They rallied their allies, forging a united front against the traitors in their midst, and prepared to confront the threat head-on.

But as they prepared to confront their enemies, they knew that the battle ahead would not be easily won. The traitors were cunning and ruthless, their thirst for power driving them to desperate lengths to maintain their grip on the settlement. And as the shadows of betrayal closed in around them,

Marcus, Kate, Rola, and their companions braced themselves for the final showdown that would determine the fate of their home—and their future.

**The Final Stand :

In the dim light of dawn, the settlement stood on the brink of chaos as Marcus, Kate, Rola, and their companions prepared to confront the traitors who threatened to tear their home apart. Tension hung heavy in the air, mingling with the acrid scent of fear and uncertainty as the survivors braced themselves for the battle ahead.

With grim determination, Marcus, Kate, Rola, and their allies assembled at the heart of the settlement, their faces set in determined expressions as they prepared to face their enemies head-on. They knew that the fate of their home—and their future—hinged on the outcome of the coming confrontation, and they were ready to fight with

every ounce of strength and
courage they possessed.

As the traitors emerged from the shadows, their faces twisted with malice and greed, Marcus, Kate, Rola, and their companions squared off against them, their weapons at the ready as they prepared to defend their home against the forces of betrayal and deceit.

The battle that followed was fierce and brutal, each side fighting tooth and nail for control of the settlement.

Swords clashed, arrows flew, and the air was filled with the screams of the wounded as the survivors clashed in a desperate struggle for survival.

Despite the odds stacked against them, Marcus, Kate, Rola, and their allies fought with a ferocity born of desperation, their determination unwavering in the face of overwhelming odds. They rallied together, their bond as a family giving them strength as they pushed back against the traitors with all their might.

But as the battle raged on, it became clear that victory would not come easily. The traitors fought with a ruthless cunning, their thirst for power driving them to ever greater acts of treachery and deceit. And as the casualties mounted and the settlement lay in ruins, Marcus, Kate, Rola, and their companions knew that they faced their greatest challenge yet.

In the end, It was not the strength of their weapons or the ferocity of their attacks that determined the outcome of the battle, but the strength of their spirit and the depth of their resolve. And as the dust settled and the smoke cleared, Marcus, Kate, Rola, and their allies emerged victorious, their home saved from destruction and their enemies vanquished once and for all.

As they stood amidst the ruins of the settlement, battered and bruised but unbowed, Marcus, Kate, Rola, and their companions knew that they had faced their greatest challenge and emerged stronger for it. And as they looked to the future, they knew that whatever trials lay ahead, they would face them together, united in their determination to rebuild their home and forge a new future from the ashes of the past.

: Rebuilding Hope**

In the aftermath of the final, grueling battle, the settlement lay in ruins, its once-sturdy walls reduced to rubble, and its streets littered with the detritus of war. But amidst the devastation, a glimmer of hope remained, as Marcus, Kate, Rola, and their companions emerged victorious, their bond as a family stronger than ever in the face of adversity.

With determination and resilience, the survivors set to work rebuilding their shattered home. They cleared away the debris, salvaged what they could, and began the arduous task of rebuilding their homes and their lives from the ground up.

Every member of the settlement contributed to the reconstruction effort, whether it was gathering building materials, repairing structures, or providing moral support to their neighbors. Despite the hardships they faced, their spirits remained unbroken, fueled by the knowledge that they were working together to create a brighter future.

As time passed, the settlement began to take shape once more. New walls rose from the ashes, stronger and more fortified than before. Gardens were planted, and homes were rebuilt, each brick laid a testament to the resilience and determination of the survivors.

But perhaps the most significant change was the sense of unity that permeated the settlement. Through hardship and loss, the survivors had forged bonds that transcended the trials they had faced. They had weathered the storm together and emerged stronger for it, their shared experiences cementing their commitment to each other and to the future they were building.

As the sun set on the newly rebuilt settlement, casting a warm glow over the horizon, Marcus, Kate, Rola, and their companions looked out over their home with pride and gratitude. Though scars remained, both seen and unseen, they knew that they had overcome the darkest of days and emerged victorious on the other side.

And as they gathered together, sharing stories and laughter amidst the ruins, they knew that no matter what challenges lay ahead, they would face them together, united in their shared resolve to rebuild, to thrive, and to never lose hope in the face of adversity.

**Rebuilding Bonds :

With the settlement's walls now restored and a renewed sense of security in the air, Marcus, Kate, Rola, and their companions set out to rebuild not just their physical surroundings but also the bonds that held them together as a community.

In the days following the victory over betrayal, the survivors came together in a spirit of unity and cooperation. They shared meals, exchanged stories, and lent each other a helping hand as they worked tirelessly to restore the settlement to its former glory.

For Marcus and Kate, the rebuilding process brought them closer together than ever before. They found solace in each other's company, drawing strength from their shared experiences and the knowledge that they had overcome seemingly insurmountable challenges as a team. With every brick laid and every wall reinforced, their love and trust in one another deepened, anchoring them firmly in the present and guiding them towards a .brighter future

Meanwhile, Rola reveled in the newfound sense of community that surrounded her. She made friends with the other children in the settlement, laughing and playing as if the horrors of the past were nothing more than distant memories. Her infectious energy brought joy to all who knew her, serving as a beacon of hope in even the darkest of times.

As the settlement began to take shape once more, Marcus, Kate, Rola, and their companions found themselves filled with a sense of pride and accomplishment. They had faced unimaginable trials and emerged victorious, their bonds stronger than ever and their spirits unbroken.

But even as they celebrated their successes, they knew that the road ahead would not be without its challenges. The world outside their walls remained a dangerous and unpredictable place, and they would need to remain vigilant in order to protect all that they had rebuilt.

As the sun set on another day in the settlement, Marcus, Kate, Rola, and their companions gathered around a crackling fire, their hearts full of gratitude for the blessings they had been given. And as they looked towards the future, they did so with renewed hope and determination, knowing that together, they could overcome anything that stood in their way.

Conclusion: Forging Ahead

As the settlement stood firm against the backdrop of a world forever changed, Marcus, Kate, Rola, and their companions reflected on the journey that had brought them to this moment.

They had faced unimaginable challenges, confronting betrayal, loss, and adversity at every turn. But through it all, they had remained resolute, their spirits unbroken and their resolve unwavering.

Now, as they looked towards the future, they did so with a sense of hope and determination. The road ahead would be long and uncertain, but they would face it together, drawing strength from the bonds of friendship and family that had sustained them through .the darkest of days

For Marcus, Kate, Rola, and their companions, the journey was far from over. But with courage in their hearts and the promise of a new beginning on the horizon, they stepped forward into the unknown, ready to embrace whatever challenges lay ahead.

And as they did, they knew that no matter what trials awaited them, they would face them with unwavering resolve, forging ahead into the future with hope, determination, and a steadfast belief in the power of the human spirit to overcome even the greatest of obstacles.

Conclusion: Forging ** **Ahead

As the settlement stood firm against the backdrop of a world forever changed, Marcus, Kate, Rola, and their companions reflected on the

journey that had brought
them to this moment.

They had faced unimaginable challenges, confronting betrayal, loss, and adversity at every turn. But through It all, they had remained resolute, their spirits unbroken and their resolve unwavering.

Now, as they looked towards the future, they did so with a sense of hope and determination. The road ahead would be long and uncertain, but they would face it together, drawing strength from the bonds of friendship and family that had sustained them through .the darkest of days

For Marcus, Kate, Rola, and their companions, the journey was far from over. But with courage in their hearts and the promise of a new beginning on the horizon, they stepped forward into the unknown, ready to embrace whatever .challenges lay ahead

And as they did, they knew that no matter what trials awaited them, they would face them with unwavering resolve, forging ahead into the future with hope, determination, and a steadfast belief in the power of the human spirit to overcome even the greatest of obstacles